Making a Circuit

Chris Oxlade

Heinemann Library
Chicago, Illinois

www.capstonepub.com
Visit our website to find out
more information about
Heinemann-Raintree books.

To order:

☎ Phone 888-454-2279

🖥 Visit www.capstonepub.com
to browse our catalog and order online.

Edited by Daniel Nunn, Rebecca Rissman, and Catherine Veitch
Designed by Joanna Hinton-Malivoire
Picture research by Elizabeth Alexander
Production by Eirian Griffiths
Originated by Capstone Global Library, Ltd.
Printed and bound in China by Leo Paper Products Ltd

15 14 13 12 11
10 9 8 7 6 5 4 3 2 1

Library of Congress Cataloging-in-Publication Data
Oxlade, Chris.
  Making a circuit / Chris Oxlade.
    p. cm.—(It's electric!)
  Includes bibliographical references and index.
  ISBN 978-1-4329-5674-5 (hb)—ISBN 978-1-4329-5679-0
(pb) 1. Electric circuits—Juvenile literature. 2. Electricity—
Juvenile literature. I. Title.
  TK148.O95 2012
  621.319'2—dc23   2011016533

Acknowledgments
The author and publisher are grateful to the following for
permission to reproduce photographs: Alamy p. 29
(© Jeff Lam); © Capstone Publishers pp. 4 (Karon Dubke),
5 (Karon Dubke), 8 (Karon Dubke), 9 (Karon Dubke), 10
(Karon Dubke), 11 (Karon Dubke), 12 (Karon Dubke), 14
(Karon Dubke), 16 (Karon Dubke), 21 (Karon Dubke), 23
(Karon Dubke), 25 (Karon Dubke); iStockphoto pp. 13
(© Jivko Kazakov), 17 (© bojan fatur); Photolibrary p, 27
(Stockbroker); Shutterstock pp. 6 (© sergioconsoli), 15
(© Shi Yali), 26 (© Elena Elisseeva), 28 (© Naturaldigital).

Cover photograph of students and a teacher in class
with an electronic project reproduced with permission
of Shutterstock (© Monkey Business Images). Design
background feature reproduced with permission of
Shutterstock (© echo3005).

The publisher would like to thank John Pucek for his
assistance in the preparation of this book.

Contents

Some words are shown in bold, **like this**. You can find them in the glossary on page 30.

Electricity and Circuits

Electricity is one of our most useful **resources**. It powers all sorts of machines, from flashlights to trains. It also lights up our homes and streets.

Electricity powers the complicated circuits in this cell phone.

When you touch the wire in this game, you make a loop that electricity can flow around. This makes a **buzzer** sound.

Electricity flows through things to make them work. But it can only flow around a loop that is complete. The loop is called an electric **circuit**.

Conductors and Insulators

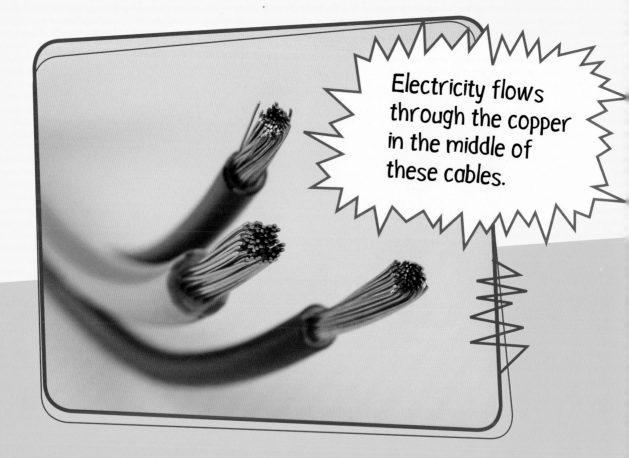

Electricity flows through the copper in the middle of these cables.

Electricity cannot flow everywhere. It can flow through some materials, but not through others. Materials that electricity can flow through are called **conductors**. Most conductors are metals.

Electricity cannot flow through most materials. These materials are called **insulators**. The plastic on the outside of a cable is an insulator. It stops electricity from escaping.

Here are some common conductors and insulators:

Conductors	Insulators
copper	plastic
iron	ceramic
steel	glass
aluminum	wood
gold	paper
silver	rubber

A Simple Circuit

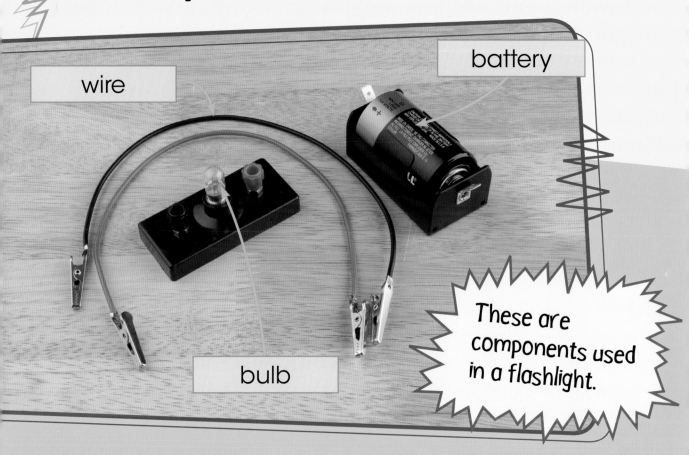

wire

battery

bulb

These are components used in a flashlight.

An electric **circuit** is made up of parts called **components**. The components are connected by wires. The electricity flows along the wires and through the components.

When components are connected together to make a circuit, electricity flows around the circuit. If there is a break in the circuit, the electricity stops flowing.

Electricity flows out of the **battery**, through the bulb and back to the battery.

Making Electricity Flow

Electricity doesn't just flow around **circuits** by itself. It needs a push to make it flow. In many things, such as flashlights and toys, the push comes from **batteries**.

Batteries push electricity around the circuits in this toy.

batteries

You can think of a battery as being like a pump for electricity. It's a bit like a water pump pushing water through a loop of a hose. The water goes around the hose and back to the pump.

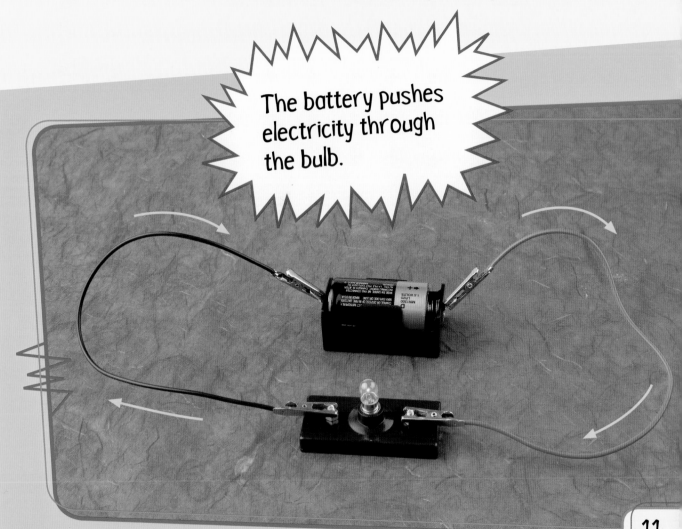

The battery pushes electricity through the bulb.

Components

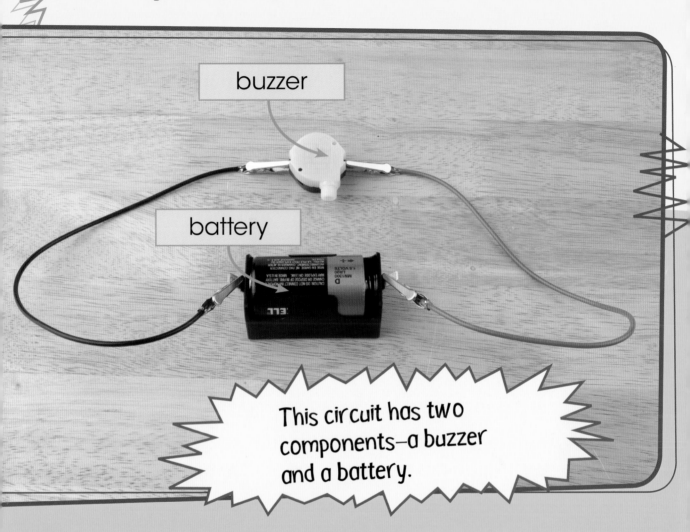

buzzer

battery

This circuit has two components—a buzzer and a battery.

Each **component** in an electric **circuit** does a job. **Batteries** and light bulbs are simple components. **Buzzers** and motors are components, too.

The circuits in machines such as televisions, radios, and computers are made up of hundreds of components. Many of the components are **microchips**.

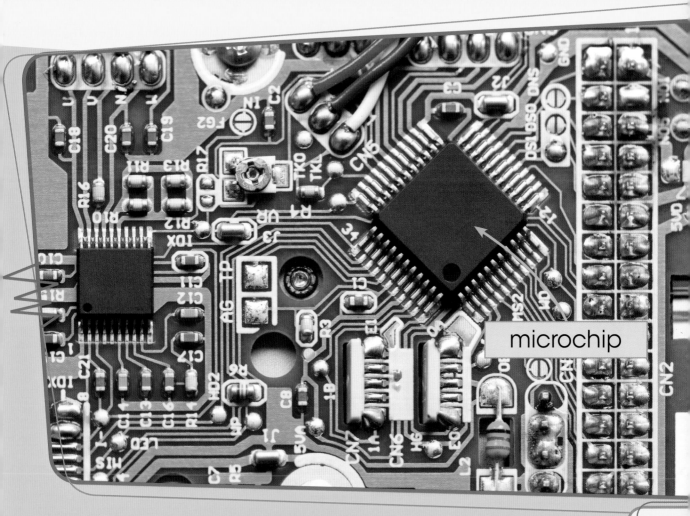

microchip

Making Connections

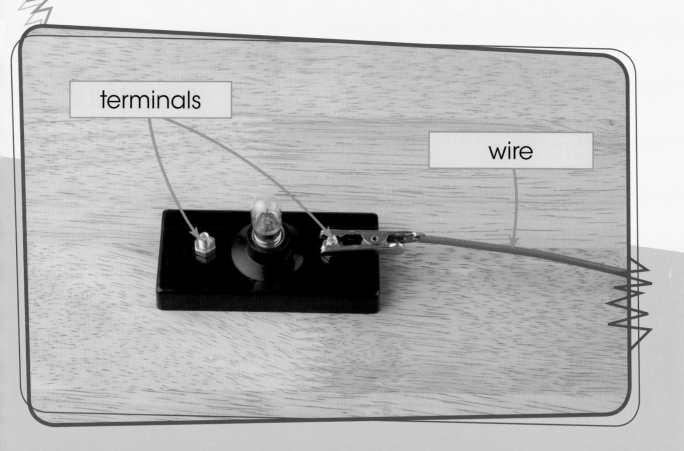

terminals

wire

The **components** in electric **circuits** need to be connected, or joined, so that electricity can flow between them. The connections between components such as **batteries** and bulbs are made with wire.

In complicated circuits, the connections are made with strips of metal on a plastic board. Most simple components have two places where wires or strips of metal connect them to a circuit. These are called **terminals**.

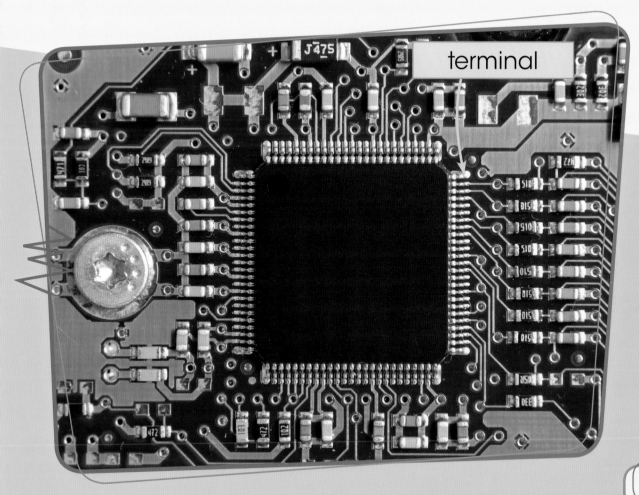

terminal

Switching On and Off

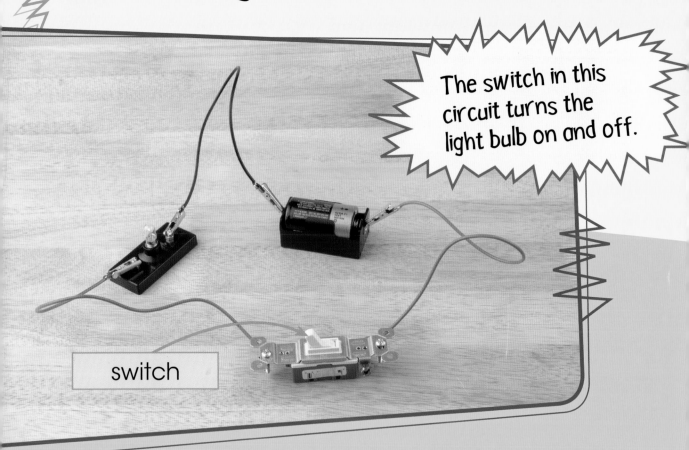

The switch in this circuit turns the light bulb on and off.

switch

Electricity only flows around a **circuit** if the circuit is a complete loop. If there is a break in the loop, the **current** stops flowing. A switch is a **component** that lets us break a circuit when we want to.

Opening a switch breaks a circuit. This stops the electricity flowing. Closing a switch completes the circuit. This lets the electricity flow again.

There are many switches inside an aircraft cockpit.

Circuit Diagrams

If you want to show somebody how to make an electric **circuit**, you can draw a picture of the circuit for them. This picture is called a **circuit diagram**. The **components** are shown by small pictures called symbols.

These are the symbols for some common components.

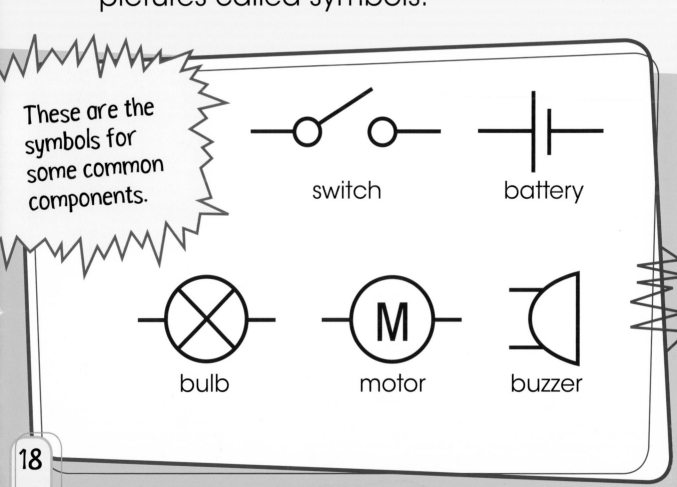

switch

battery

bulb

motor

buzzer

To draw a circuit diagram, you draw the symbols for the components in the circuit. Then you draw lines to show how the components are connected to each other.

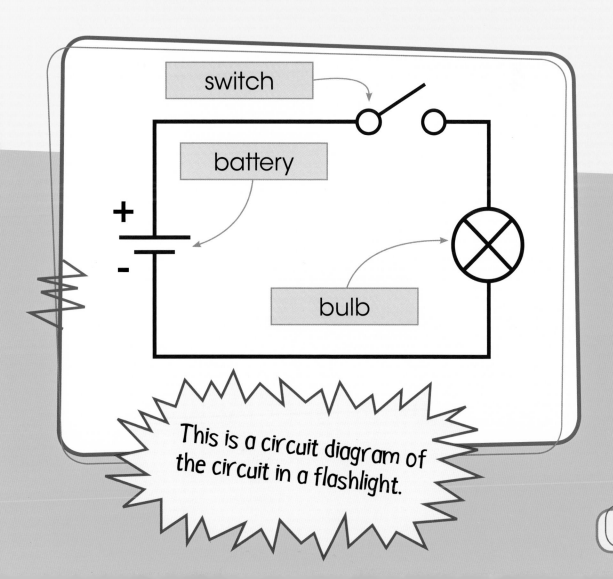

switch

battery

+

-

bulb

This is a circuit diagram of the circuit in a flashlight.

Building a Circuit

Can you tell what components are in this circuit?

You can make a **circuit** by studying a **circuit diagram**. First you work out what **components** you need to make the circuit. You do this by looking at the symbols.

When you have found the components you need, you arrange them in the same way as they are in the diagram. The lines in the diagram show you how to connect the components together.

This circuit was made using the diagram on the opposite page.

Series and Parallel

Series **circuits** and parallel circuits are two types of circuits. In a series circuit, all the **components** are in one loop. The electricity flows through one component, then the next, until it gets back to where it started.

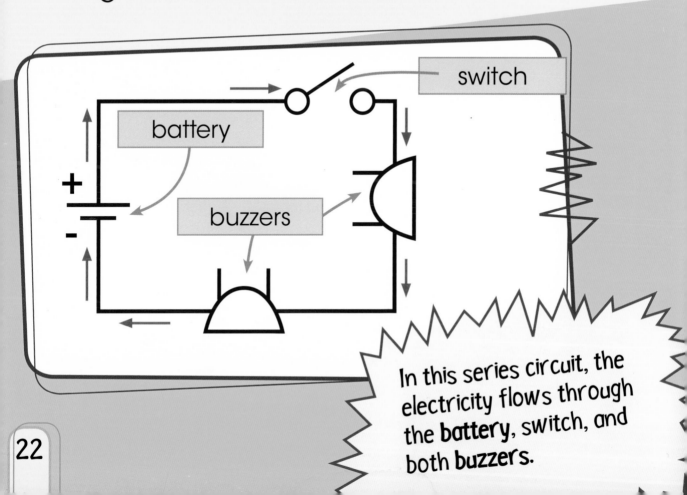

switch

battery

buzzers

+

-

In this series circuit, the electricity flows through the **battery**, switch, and both **buzzers**.

The electricity flows through one bulb, then the other.

You can add a new component to a series circuit. Then all the electricity flowing in the circuit goes through the new component, too. If you put two bulbs in series, they are only half as bright as one bulb.

In a parallel **circuit** the electricity splits up and goes different ways. Some of the electricity takes one path through the circuit. Some takes a different path through the circuit.

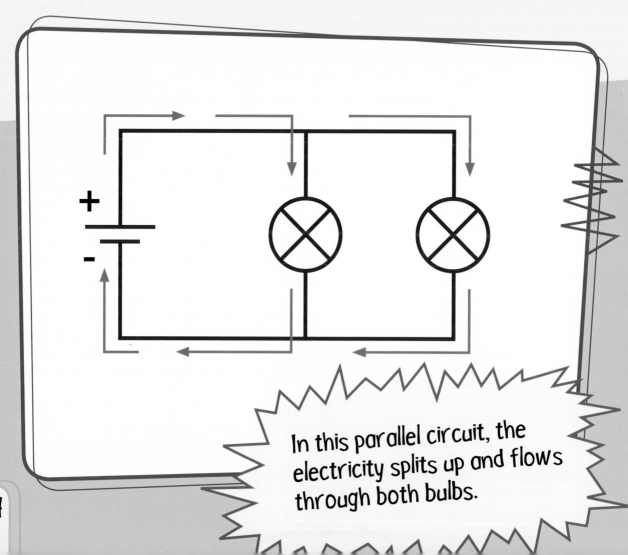

In this parallel circuit, the electricity splits up and flows through both bulbs.

You can add a new **component** to a parallel circuit. Then some of the electricity flowing in the circuit flows through the new component, too. If you put two bulbs in parallel, the electricity splits up and flows through both bulbs.

Both bulbs light up.

Household Circuits

An appliance is plugged into an outlet and becomes part of the circuit.

There are electric **circuits** in homes. The circuits are buried in the walls and floors. They carry electricity to wall outlets. When you plug in an appliance, such as a toaster, into an outlet, the appliance becomes part of the circuit.

There are circuits that carry electricity to the lights in your home. There are switches in the circuits. When you flip a light switch, a circuit is completed, and the light bulb comes on.

This electrician is putting electric circuits into a home.

Safety with Circuits

The electricity that flows in household **circuits** is very powerful. If it goes through a person, it can badly injure him or her. It can even kill. Never push anything into an electrical outlet or into a light fixture.

Danger
High voltage

⚠ 21308 KD

Warning signs show us that electricity is dangerous.

Most household circuits have a special safety feature. It's called a **circuit breaker**. If something goes wrong with the circuit or somebody gets an electric shock, the circuit breaker switches off the electricity.

Circuit breakers save lives by switching off electricity in an emergency.

Glossary

battery part that pushes electricity around a circuit

buzzer part that makes a buzzing sound when electricity flows through it

circuit loop that electricity flows around

circuit breaker safety part that switches off electricity if something goes wrong

circuit diagram diagram that shows how the parts in a circuit are connected

component something that does a job in an electric circuit, such as a battery or a bulb

conductor material that electricity can flow through

current flow of electricity through a wire or circuit

insulator material that electricity cannot flow through

microchip small part that contains a very complicated electric circuit

resource something that we use for making things and living our lives

Find Out More

Books

Oxlade, Chris. *Electricity (Investigate)*. Chicago: Heinemann Raintree, 2008.

Royston, Angela. *Conductors and Insulators (My World of Science)*. Chicago: Heinemann Raintree, 2008.

Spilsbury, Louise and Richard. *Circuits and Conductors*. New York: M. Evans, 2006.

Websites

http://kids.librarypoint.org/simply_circuits
Circuits and more at this website.

http://scifiles.larc.nasa.gov/text/kids/ Problem_Board/problems/electricity/ circuits2.html
Learn more about circuits from NASA.

Index